A Voice in
the Wilderness

A Voice in the Wilderness

New and Selected Poems

Mathew Tenon

Quercus Books   Palo Alto   2006

To purchase a copy of *A Voice in the Wilderness,*
send a check for $25, which includes postage and handling,
to Sue Kemp, 271 Seale Avenue, Palo Alto, California 94301.

CONTENTS

Part I
FIDELITIES
Odes

Part II
THE HOUSE OF THE BELOVED
Psalmic Cantos

Part III
HEARD IN THE NIGHT
A Nearness

Part I

Fidelities

Odes

First Ode

In the midst of all my
Getting and my doing comes
Something into me that cares not
Of the getting and the doing.
A calm with its own quiet harmony,
Existing without struggle or violence,
Preserving a floating hub
In the wheel of things.
It comes and I feel it.
Yet I cannot grasp or touch it more
Than I can touch the sunlight.
It touches me, and I am content.

Second Ode

Now I begin to feel the sun of understanding,
How it glows and wakens me.
It opens me and fills my darkness
And sweeps away my sleeping angers and idles.
Now I strive to know.
The clearing shafts enter a hungry mind
Where once they beat upon skin.
My eyes were glazed against them and were
Only for the steps of the treadmill.
The distance from step to step
Is small and narrow.
But the measures from pillar to pillar
In the gardens of understanding are many times great
And are not filled with feet.
The colors of life live in this sun.
They work upon my earth
And bring many
Flowers before the good fruit.
The treadmill turns still but it
Is gone from my thoughts,
For my thoughts have come out
Of the churning.
I shall delight in my time
And keep a bright watch.

Third Ode

May the love large and kind
Increase in me this day.
May it rise up and run into
The blood of my nature
Like a precious liquor.
May it run among my thoughts
And multiply.
May it spill my measure
And make a sweet smell in my fire.
The world about me is changed.
And the days are made more rich
And a way is cleared
In the confusion.
My fire flickers, yet
The aroma wakens me.
It makes me stronger than my limbs,
It makes me supple as the glove
And to take comfort in what can be.
I shall cherish it and breathe its names.

Fourth Ode

I arise from cool slumbers
To go and set my sail upon
The untrod water.
What little reckoning I hold
Will serve as compass well enough.
My sinews are tender yet I trust
Them more than a mooring of precious
Metal for they grow with trial.
If no breeze waits for me at the door
I shall go and find one to set
My blade across.
The rise and fall
Of the swell gives pleasure.
It rocks me and plays into my
Thoughts and being with its travel.
My blood responds and my
Cells keep the time of their life
And the time and beat messaged to them.
Perhaps I shall catch
One or two of the lines that reflect
In the trackless waters.
They sometimes show themselves through
The watery clarity.
I shall take them up
As reins upon a gentle sea horse
And sense their traces
Among the currents.

My sail is as myself,
No better, no worse.
Free to raise at will,
Supple to lighten and furl,
Worn as expected,
Many times soiled
And many times sun-washed and whitened.
The people are elusive as
The fishes of the water
And the birds of the air.
Some swooping to look at me,
Some veering off, some fearful.
Some laughing at me, I laughing in return.
Many more beautifully
Marked and smoother.
Many seeming molded and made
For their element better than I.
Some are rough looking and large,
Others are deer-eyed.
Some confident and fine.
Some troubled.
All glide by hardly looking my way.
Some seem open and good humored,
Some soft as doves, some seem hostile.
Yet the multitude would
Have but a look hurriedly taken
And speed on
While I continue my course,
Being fully alive and of good cheer,

Bobbing a bit of color over the deep.
And the great body of human
Fishes and birds go about their
Matters with a busy, nodding
And sometimes sulky acquaintance.
And my sail sails on
Hailing them and wishing them well,
And finding harbor in many strange places.

Fifth Ode

The hours rush on and I think of them.
What came of them? Where is my gain?
And yet, why weigh time so?
Do I live in my pockets?
Have I forgotten the get of life is never enough?
Or perhaps the spell of the get and count
Has stilled my senses.
It is a donkey plod and my being has
Fallen asleep on little feet.
Fitness and understanding set the world turning
And this is the motion to wake with
The stride and love of life,
Catching up life itself for its own sake,
For the strange winding and unwinding,
Curiously stumbling into hidden dramas
Of ants and men tugging
On the stems and ropes of things.
Not for acceptance but wonder,
Not for closures
But openings,
Nor for thin speed
But for the large life,
Life that walks off the burning
Highway of get and get and get
And pauses to look around,
Finding there is no need to burn intensity,
When there is awareness,

Noticing how the sight of awareness sees
The shades and telltale ways of things.
Yes, I shall go now and stretch my being,
Striding out with a light and easy sway.
My life grows larger
And extends beyond me.
I pause and look about
Spending time by a new clock.
Then move slowly on,
Breaking open the shells of experience.

Sixth Ode

Let me go now and search among
The strange and beautiful faces
For I want to be lost from myself a while
Down the avenue down from Alberta wheatfields
And the air of meadowlarks striding limber
And easy a manly fellow of broad open face
Full-meeting my eyes, well nourished
And fit in fresh laundered clothes. High noon
Shines through his sandy cropped hair, a man
Not scattered in pieces but whole.
A woman who walks in lillies of the moon
Approaches, distant dulcet of hollowing cheeks
A fine white powder suspended in her gaze.
How strangely beautiful to see her
Moving next to a spare man
Tall in a hard body that shines the patina
Of light rubbed leather, the reined cords
Of his neck drawn taut, his cheeks
Burnished in the sun like shields.
Behind them in fast tack a clicking stepper
Of San Juan style scattering a trail of music
And glances through the platinum pale
Of the girl from Sweden as she questions
Herself and her snow-ringed hours
Where frail archers of light
Shoot into drifts of lemon green mist.
Now a young fellow who must feed

On cactus thorn and lizards' tails and yet
Hearing says there is a brilliant tenderness
Behind the smooth hair and high cut nostrils.
No sooner gone than a face of white wine
Turning away in a faint smile of silver veils
And gray evening. The air of sylphs
Is not so rare, she moves yet waits in it.
Now comes an invisible face never showing
A flicker of the marked intelligence within,
A hundred guesses will not catch
The train in her thought for it goes
On disappearing tracks.
Now a bloating face of lumps of starch
And malted eyes looking down
Passing out the starts of apologies.
Here come a pair of happy eyes
Swimming and laughing with some quirked
Story that lifts thin time up
And makes it plump.
Here a face of charted success that looks
Long at figures and never wanders from
What is right ahead, handsome clothed in gray
Red on weekends. In close behind a girl
Of eager-mouthed expectation, dart eyes
Hair struck in place forever,
The very nose of anxious confidence set
On a certain trail.
Following her a surf of frothing green breaks
In this woman's jasper eyes beached in fair

Complexion well sanded with tiny strawberries
Her coral ears laid back tight
And seeming not to hear.
Angelfish have lost their
Way in these eyes among swift glances
And spears damascened in gold,
The easy curling lips drop soft accents
And honeysuckles; poppies and oranges play
In her brow netted and swept
By free streams of dark hair.
And here at the corner a sudden girl
Freckled with wild rice, her long arms
Overflown with chestnut hair as they
Talk and jerk in articulate angles.
Carefully edging along the windows a walking
Parchment of intense study and precision,
His hair a close-hugging brown moss
Knots of wood spreading in the cheeks
Diamond eyes that seem to crack
The glass they look in.
There cheekbones that could be Shawnee
Or Sioux or out of earliest times.
The large mouth firmly drawn from
A drum stretched over centuries of sundowns
Rain and fire a jaw hammered
Out of fish scales and buffalo.
Slipping through them all the jag-toothed
Grin of a taunter escaped from school,
A punch of momentary plays

And heavy-curtained frowns
A whirl of yellow jasmine has caught his arm
And he's off in both directions
And untouched in high stoned air.
And here is a face of pox and fried creases smiling
Loyally with buckteeth and rusty wire eyebrows.
And here walks the plainest of the plain
Speaking wordlessly of a quiet home shy
Love and faithfulness.
Now one of sulk and brooding, coal mines sunk
Deep in her eyes and crushed rubies
Smoking on her lips.
The slender African antelope girl has the neck
Of a silver ewer, her lightly parted lips
Glow softly like ancient red sealstones.
Long bronze forks of her brother's
Keen glances reach far down the block
As he glides by, his body showing a frame
Of delicate bone in fine clear line.
Here close a little girl of new ivory with her
Mother of old ivory
Slow-paced in a painful gait, her throat
Puffing and clucking all the while.
From Hawaii a richly fleshed woman of carnelian
Tints dusted over with the mocha
Of butterfly wings, her large rounded chin
Blooming in cinnamon and almonds.
And there a crumpled paper bag face, slow eyes
Squeezing and squinting out of

A map of troubles perhaps never traveled.
Here is a bright brick face that might have
Lived off Galway Bay, the blue marble gaze
Staring out over a sea of sentiment surging
And rippling among friends loves and rivals.
There bobs a bouncing ball of a boy's head
Full of jiggling question marks
Mock challenge and shrill calls.
The tense sinuous hand
There pointing in the window could be
Italian or is it a newer blend?
Now he deftly touches his companion's
Necklace round an alabaster
Neck more lovely than white,
The air about her momentary still seems
Crystalline and shimmering with roses and limes.
Looking on, the featureless clouded face
Of a young girl seeming already
Silenced and resigned, yet is it so?
At the last crossway a fierce
Deep-hacked face saying knowing encouraging
Words to an old woman, starting prickles
In her withered eyes,
Proving the easy guesses wrong again.

Seventh Ode

I cry out to our sacred spirit
To take up
The anguish within me.
To give heed and enter
My clots and ferment.
I cry out without words
From the depths of me.
Surely it will find my grief.
Surely it will lift
With its strong easing fingers
And sweeten my bitterness.
Let it come now and comfort me.
Let it moisten my hide
And send drink to the fibers
Of my strength and my courage.
I bend down, yet out of this
Shall I be nourished and drawn up
To greater measure as the fertile
Field beats down yet
Takes drink under the storm.
And the morning shall be new,
The rain shall sweep away.

Eighth Ode

Our love beareth flowers each day,
Of deep purpling reds
Of happiest yellows, of clear-eyed
Blues, and of a white serene.
And each day we give these
Flowers carelessly, in rich profusion,
Over the heave and breadth of the day,
Expecting no return,
Hoping to be left with few to fade
And waste their scent and seed.

Ninth Ode

Look, look, eyes open wide
Large and new-waked set this
A watching time as stepping aside
From my self I come alive in you in seeing and tear
The curtain from the play
Of life in this very act in which we stand.
Freed from what it means
To me, catching cues and hints
Of what it is to those who scamper
And totter across the earthy stage.
We peer and listen
Taking life from life itself.
These are dramas done by
The only perfect actors performing
Not a remembered art but their own in
Acts and lines that show the ways of life.
Now untied reality ravels out its fresh script
Gazing into the life of sudden instants
Men and women before half-seen as
Cardboard figures
Now begin to round, seeming larger with their own
Story strands weaving, crossing.
Now none goes unheeded and none is
Trimmed down to good or bad.
All judgments are suspended,
It is the time to see not to judge,
To question not to answer,

To feel the human current
And send balloons
Of wonder up above the shadows of ourselves.
The moments come forward
Cut from the ties that held them
In old bundles.
Moments too true and oddly ordinary
To be told in tales,
Feelings that were never named,
Flashes that are quenched
Dried and flattened when preserved.
Alive, one scene teems a book
Of storied cause and meaning
Masked and unmasked
I ask whence comes this posture,
This flicker, the curling smile
That swallowed word, that nod.
What is the meaning
Of that hand movement
Who swims behind those eyes,
What is the old cause of this look now?
Looking deeply, the bone that castles the mind
Is guessed, the wish that turns the act,
The shadowed rest that set free a sigh.
Yes there is everywhere to see
Worlds that never meet the busy eye.
Though I did sightsee the cities, yet until
I caught a sight of men and women I was
Home in bed for they have more streets

And byways than the globe can carry on its back.
Life will tell the observer;
To others life is mum.

Tenth Ode

Through years of the days and days
Storied to follow laws of good conduct.
My voice sounded template
And seemed fair with its words. And I struggled to
Live according to right ways
And did a good share.
There were not many who found
Fault in my ways or words
For I tried to pass.
I had good times and
The nags of behavior I quieted and I
Escaped much trouble. But there was
No more. For life was ruled small
And gave little juice. I became thirsty,
Then I turned about
And came to do such things
Not so much for the following as
The good that comes of them
Beyond the hour and the day,
Sometimes appearing unnoticed
In a life close to mine
Or in my own, or
Touching those I would never know,
Or hear in a new brood of children
Far off, even after death.
I kept no watch nor
Wait for their result

And was content for them
To work unseen and imperfectly,
Sometimes falling by the way when
Hardly begun. And then there came
Happiness in these things.

Eleventh Ode

My love left me in the cold night
And I was chilled and sick at heart.
Like the breath of caves
Loneliness came over me.
My time had stopped.
And the dampness
Of earth
Entered me as into one buried.
But then a far off flickering fire,
Crept into my eyes.
Then another and another
Along the road, beyond the dim hill, as far
As I could see, strewn carelessly
As from a vast sweeping arm.
I looked long in silence and sadness,
Hardly knowing light or dark
Or their parting.
And then I guessed they were
The scattered fires of love.
And I saw they were growing larger.
Larger and brighter and yet
More red, making islands in the black
Sky to move and blush.
The flames waxed and grew and rose up
In tumultuous towers until the islands ran
Together and all the sky was blood red
And streaked and the air about me was warmed.

Then it was crimson and swelled with swirling
Streams of yellow and thick grey until the earth
And the air above became a soundless inferno.
The roofs of houses shone and glistened brightly
And the tops of trees swayed and hurled
To and fro like flames on shifting winds
And they become not red but
Writhing green and grew taller.
Water ran down their trunks in silver
Torrents like sliding films of ice
Yet the leaves were dry.
Swallows flew up out of their roosts
And circled and hovered with strange ease
Their eyes becoming soft and large.
The sky could become no more red and was
Nearing bruised purple and black.
Suddenly white sheets of rain fell into
The inferno as though they were nothing.
Then there was a cooling and a gentle trembling
Rain prevailed and after a time it slowed
And then the high spirit swept through
Me and told me to take my
Little coal of love and make it many.
To take it that was narrow and make
It large and kindly.
Then I saw the inferno
Was gone away and it was peaceful.
And the little fires came up
One by one and comforted me.

I saw that my skin was not
Scorched but moist. And my heart was
Swelled and my vision was clearing.
I said I will take my love in little
Twigs and cast them into the struggling fires.
I will plant embers where there are none.

Twelfth Ode

Take my home, my flagged steps
And my favorite chair
The sun-drinking window on the open road
My hemlock and my yellow cat,
Take them, they are more than I can carry.
I am not finished.
Yes the antique table for my
Tobacco and books, the nearness of friends
The old fashioned cups that talk
To one who lives alone,
Take them, so long as I may
Keep bright hail for experience.

Thirteenth Ode

My heart shall grow large
Large as a melon of the vine fresh cut
That spills a little.
Full and shining with seed and juice
For I would not have it a puckered
Lemon drying in my cabinet.
Large with greening hopes
And fresh remembrances,
With passing slights and chills that freeze
The air to a skyless bullring, with flying
Hooves dark lashes and lustrous eyes,
With blazed angers and smoldering wantings
And ashen fear. With the pale girl in her
Hospital bed and her slow-sinking eyes,
The full contralto voice as it climbs
Above the whiteness of the bride and her
Mate standing still and close.
The little child who peeped in my
Face and was carried away,
With twining thoughts spun along the sidewalk
Traceless as a puff of dust,
The delicious aroma of burning leaves,
Curious glances from park benches,
The fleshy molds of passing beauty,
The intent faces of lovers carefully
Unwrapping solitary words.
With the potent heavy-laden

Shelves of books in the great carved library
And the cool new library shaped only
Of angles and light.
Out of the aura that streams from admired
Men and women, and the fiber and tenacity
Of an unbreakable one fighting a losing battle.
With the blood-soaked newspapers telling
Of war begetting war and the sullen
Disgust for the promotion of violence.
From the relentless press of eyes through
The cage of the passing prison van,
And the sparks off the teeth of the one who
Has no secret names of death.
The laughing jeer of the tenement
Woman who knows well enough,
Her red puffed ankles edging over the curb.
With the shy flicker of friendliness hovering
In the look of the stranger,
With the shine of the dark suit carefully
Pressed again, and the ebb and flow of a dress
On a well formed figure. With the supple play
Of young bodies on the winnowing sand,
The caress of the sea's foaming fingers
About my feet and the kiss of the breeze
On the back of my neck.
The pure fresh-swept air from
The north and the west, the miraculous fires
Of the sinking sun, the return homeward
Past windows gleaming in the dusk.

With the robin's low call over the shadowed lawn
And the calm power of the darkening pines,
With the mysteriously gathering
Veil enfolding murmuring faces, with linen
Visions and soft repose.
The last payment of rent and the troubled
Move from home,
The dusty floors of empty rooms
And the cramping squeeze of shrinking scope.
With the shudder and then the slow burning.
The sudden contempt for old
Comforts and the longing for motion
And fitness. The eagerness to take on
Whatever comes. The outward-curving sweep
Of the open road. The rise and surge
Of confidence over all doubts.
The passage through the rich green divide
Breathing sun-warmed glades of laurel and grass.
The stop unobserved near
The family at the picnic table
Watching the spread of food being laid out
And the bend of the mother over
The cooing infant.
With the defiant face of the boy marched
To his father, the vague answers
To simple questions. The lingering start onward
And the arrival so welcome at the farm
Splattered over the floor of the valley.
With the burst of full-risen morning sun

And patches of bright laughter,
The song and hum of the young housewife
At work in the kitchen,
The child's wail of burned fingers
And the swift scold. The clearness and good
Health of the spinster standing
In her garden far from the main road,
The fragrant lake of cool air
At the edge of the wood, the plump
Hollow gurgle of the brook beneath
Dripping banks. Out of bits of me
Clinging to a black twig as it winds
And twists in the orb of the pool,
The glittering eyes of the schoolgirl
Surprised at her desk,
The scent of warm lilac drifting
Over the windowsill. The memory of empty letters,
The whispering depths of loneliness, the pause
Beneath the delicate lace of locust leaves
Standing in pure receptiveness.
The quiet wake of passionless memories.
The startling crack of tree limbs
Under the bulldozer's steel
Tread, the retreat of nature
Bleeding fresh earth and poisoned springs,
The twining suckers of disease, the helpless
Wait, the brief words of the surgeon
And the opening made in the dream.
With sealing words to one so long a friend

And the sudden handclasp of manly vigor.
The laughter and good times of gathered kin,
The plump hand of the baby weakly beating
And pressing my cheek.
The half-promise made to brown eyes
Patiently waiting, the words finding the mark
Well hidden in the foliage of myself.

Fourteenth Ode

How good it is when we strive together
And deal peacefully with one
Another making generous expressions
Of ourselves and our trust.
We shall use this life well
For why should we torture it?
It goes best with those who
Nourish it and learn its ways.
Our passions and our
Acts are turned to things of peace and use,
And rarely need we call the laws
Or count hairs between us.
Sometimes we pause and listen,
Hearing the voices of others.
Each with his or her own
Strangeness bringing our
Senses to life.
We see that no apologies are needed,
That the earth bears many minds
And builds and colors in generous profusion.
We see that the differences and contrasts
Are enrichments of life
And make it more than
A little trail.
We look about us, reaching beyond
Ourselves and become more free.
So, trying and blending

The known and the new
Taking in the oddities and sting
And sweetness of others, our
Lives become larger than our own
And we discover the earth and feel it home.

Part II

The House of the Beloved

Psalmic Cantos

Canto One

Seek you the pillar of security
In your house?
Seek you the lock of security
In your labor?
Seek you the embrace of security
In your beloved?
Seek you the sinews of it in meat,
And the everlasting thread in cloth?
Seek you stronghold but in these?
Stop then.
Wait.
Take time to look away.
For it is as much made within you
And of what you take into your spirit.

Canto Two

Each may give a part of himself
And that part shall be without price.
If he gives with labor
He may give his labor
If he gives with talent
He may give his talent
If he be vigilant he may give his vigil,
So also with the lightning
And sweat of his brains,
And beyond such things
Beyond the common tasks or the dearest blood
Something more shall be given —
Full and overflowing.
Neither drought nor spring nor
Sand grits shall dry it up,
Nor good fortune nor ill nor ease,
It shall be as the deepest well.
Whosoever gives in this kind rises,
Even if those who stand near him fail him.

Canto Three

Beautifully simple and yet astounding,
Richly modest,
And yet so fearlessly free,
Seed of trust, bone of character,
Such is honesty.
This plain yet glinting quality brings
A vigor and purity among us,
Moving and staying many things
To keep open the ways.
Appearing boldly or in
Gentle voice it speaks a certain
Native tongue long bred
In the heart and reason of men and women
For it is that all beings at once or at last
Look up to the clean ones,
And though they know it not
They give them praise even as
They speak of distant things.
And this they feel though they hear it not,
Sensing it in the light of life, in the life
Loved, in life enduring.

Canto Four

Not the grief of the deep sunken heart
Nor the wild grief of flesh torn out
Nor the tired grief of the ages
But each is by a way
Where grief cannot follow,
And the grieved cry
Out and ache for it aloud
For they know not where it is.
For they knew not where it is.
Cry no more, grieving one,
Hide away no more,
It lives all about you now,
At your hand
And by your side.

Canto Five

That you may be saved from crushing
Your breast, give.
That you may be rich in spirit, give.
Give of what you would take,
Give of what you cry out for,
And know of giving in anguish.
With gentleness, destroy the fear
Of an iron world.
Give wisely, give not whatsoever
Is asked, there are parasites many
And many that are made weak.
And soften not another's strength
That you may gain the pleasure of giving,
Have vision in your giving.
Give brightly.
And give out of the lode of yourself,
For if you give only of alms
If you give only of money
If you give only of things
What have you given?
What if a man draw out
A hair from his head and give it?
But what if he draw out
A piece of himself and give this?
Take pleasure in the sacrifice.
The pruned tree of fruit is most healthy,

And so the fruit created.
Give creatively,
And you shall have meaning.

Canto Six

Even as the gentle night enfolds
The weary day, so shall I bring sweet sleep
To thee. In a mantle of tenderness I bring thee
Rest and blow out the fires in thine eyes.
Moving in the forest of thy thoughts
Among the leafy hopes and murmuring
Springs, in the dimming light of thine eyes,
Shaded there, patiently holding
The slackening line, I slip the knots,
Letting fall lavish coils in the slumbrous air.
Peace for thy heart and thy tousled
Forehead I bring, with merciful quiet
Fresh liniments and forgetfulness.
Though you did lose me in the day
Yet have I returned to you faithfully.
Lo, I hang dewy crystals upon
Thy eyelids and touch thy cheeks
With soft sighs of peace.
The richest gardens are so bedded and tended,
Even as the lap of the silvery lake this peacefulness.
Come, steep thy limbs in ease
And blessed heaviness. Droop thy head upon thy
Bed and I will pour soft hours over thee,
Making a bath of charmed humors and dissolving
Thoughts to lap about thy slumbers
Come, be hushed with kindness.
Take the fold of the dreamy cloak.

The blue mountains of sleep are
Sinking with their gentle power.
Soon the gleaming clasp melts
And then at least in cool sleep
Thou shalt leave me, yet I not thee.

Canto Seven

Suffer no man to lose faith in himself,
For he that loses faith
In himself has a deep sickness,
His guts hang loose in him
And he mortifies
And sinks down.
Give courage and cheer to the broken
And the sick at heart.
Help them to gather themselves up and take new
Faith in themselves,
For they may be transformed.

Canto Eight

Then at times
Go from friends
And walk among the sunken
The unfortunate and the poor.
Seek them to rub against you
And to widen your eyes.
Talk against none
Nor think against any of them,
But take their part inwardly
Reaching into their trials
And their lacks.
Then go, and remember them,
And keep a part of them.

Canto Nine

There comes a time when you see yourself
As one down and broken.
But you have forgotten,
You have forgotten you are
A being of many successes
Proving you, and only now this
That engulfs you.
There is something of you
You cannot see,
Something both calming
And freshening
Perhaps you sometimes sense
This spirit though you cannot
Imagine its form or substance,
At moments unsuspected
It enters your actions
Powerful and penetrating,
Creating dominations and energies,
This without setting a ripple
In your memory.
It is always with you,
It is with you even now,
Be confident. Let it advance.

Canto Ten

The rock is made soft,
The water hardened,
The sheep is swallowed
And made to a finger,
And the ship got into a bottle.
So all things may be made
To the purpose.
The boldness and the gentleness
The heard and the unheard,
The sleep and the wake,
The keen and the dull.
The offense, the chastisement,
The struggle, the acquiescence,
The wealth and the want,
The clarities and the mysteries,
The song and the silence.
The beat of the heart
And the rest of the heart,
The love and the aversion,
The time of the rising up
And the time of the falling,
The tension, the ease,
The flaw and the perfection,
And the plunge and the wait;
The moment and the life.

Canto Eleven

Not as a locked still likeness,
Nor slice in tender duty bonds,
Nor as a caged bird shrunken
And waiting hold the young one.
But high perched
On the raised up arm,
That it may go as a messenger
And a piece of your heart
Full and free sent out.
Crush it no more,
The young breast sucks and aches
To taste the air of the world
And the rush of fresh breath
Out the curious nostrils.
See how the wheeling world
Sweeps up the young one
In its mantle, drawing it out to strength and life,
Making it new companions and new work
And tempting it to travels
Of seeing and learning
And sometimes full round again and home.

Canto Twelve

Keep peace with him you call enemy,
Talk with him and find his heart.
He is hid there in the darkness,
In the murmuring and the pounding,
In the closing and the squeezing
And the trembling and the hardening.
If his heart be a fearful heart
Give it ease of reason,
If it be a blind gray muscle
That knows nothing but
Work and will, draw it out,
If it be shrunken and away
Feed it and avail it,
If it be greedy
Be careful and strong.
But if his heart be hid
In the shadow of your light
What of your light
And the reflections of it.
The pulse of him, the core
The chambered psyche,
They are there in their own
Strains and songs.
Search then, find the Rosettas
And keep peace with him
For if you war upon him
And conquer him then you must still have

Peace with him.
You cannot have comfort
In your heart without peace,
Nor can you have peace
Given hardship and oppression,
For oppression will find
The heart and haunt it
And grow sores there.
And the festering is fed
By the best in you and borne up
In your gorge even by your loved ones,
And there is no lasting peace in you until you give up
And make it decent.
In the mirror comes
The face of the stranger,
And in the little children
Wait the faces of the dissatisfied.

Canto Thirteen

May the white of your rightness tumble
In gentle folds down among the fertile green,
That righteousness be
Not a sterile thing upon you
And whosoever comes near.
Rise up, yea, rise up with rightness
Yet not so high as to pass over
In cold fumes and storms, breaking
Lightning bolts on the weak,
Or in cold steel armor
White lipped and stiff in pride.
Let not the color and juice be
Squeezed out of you.
The press of life makes wine
And the cloth of life
Is white but a moment
And soon spattered on the cleanest road.

Canto Fourteen

As you give respect and kindness to a friend
So give it to the stranger,
Not alone the good and the thankful
But the eagles and the sparrows
That scratch about,
And the ugly and the sharp-tongued.
How often they are born to no decent home
And taste no warming milk
And are chill for it.
This kindness is not given for safekeep
But to be lost and swallowed up
And made part of the other.
A few sips, a little cup, even if
But a drop is spared,
It has a melting touch
And the nourishments
Of a never-soured milk.
Then why spared
Or metered out or weighed?
Is this the dividing of a last drop?
No, it is more as the spilling of a spring
For generous respect encourages goodness and decency.
Who gives this gentle juice
Becomes richer of it and made full.
And life is not bare but fruitful.

Canto Fifteen

Thy voice shall reach me for I am
Thy high spirit and about thee always.
My cloak is of love and wisdom and out of the folds of
Deliverance my hand is stretched forth.
And it comes again like the sound
Of a voice born of the green mountains,
As the fresh brook that goes down to the prairie
Flooding forth over dry land with
The rippled strength of a youth's arm.
I charge thee not in fear
But in kindness. I shall not shake fright
Before thee for I lead thee away from troubles.
What fury have I that am for thee?
I that am carried as the scent of flowers.
I speak of life not of fantasy. Therefore
Reality and plainness cannot destroy me
For I am with reality and plainness.
The world is not cheap and the neverland
A marvel,
The living reality is
Here at hand and can be made
Good and of full happy hours.
Nor do I ignore the urge and purpose
Of the flesh but give light and life to it.
I am out of thee and thy brothers and sisters
Not out of nothing and therefore am not sterile.
I take thee through pain and through the bright hours

Of joy and laughter
Never to abandon thee in a ditch of penance.
When you run into the ditch how long should be
Wallow and woe? I am a lifter for thee
And float as a white cloud rich in the run,
And I have as much truth in the light
As in the dark for my coverlet is like snow
To keep thee clean and warm, not to keep thee
In darkness and apart from men and women.
I shall show thee home among every kind
For I care for all nations and races,
And for the white, the black, the brown
And the beautiful shifting shades and the pink
Youth and grey age for they are all
Brothers and sisters one to another.
Therefore do I abhor hate and bigotry.
When brothers and sisters tear one
Another they are less than wild beasts.
In the power of justice I move among men and women
And yet I sweep the ground when the truth
Lies there, even when it lies with confusion
And foulness, I take the dust
That is ground by the cruel heel and make it
A mud to splatter and stick to him,
And I shall be like a changing power to him
That he cannot find my arms.
I shall turn again and again
To make peacefulness and goodness prevail.
Then again I am like a loving father.

The eyes of my head are set in kindness
And my arm and my scapula are formed of courage.
Love is the blood of my veins.
When you fall into the well
Of loneliness reach for my hand
And I shall draw thee up.
Come to me when you are troubled
And I shall comfort thee.
Come to me when you are struck down
And I will give thee strength.
Come to me when you are joyous
And I will take nourishment from thee
And multiply thy quality.
The wind scatters the good seed with abandon
And the machine scatters the seed with precision
But I ruffle thee and plant thee lovingly
For I would keep thee from becoming
A machine of dead life.
I nourish the womb and semen
Of thy goodness, and every good thing you do
And every happy thing you do gives me
Food and drink. Yet when thine eyes
Would fix my body they pass
Through me clean like a sun ray in the water cup.
Still am I there as the drink for life
To make thee an enjoyer of life
Not only an enjoyer of the exalted.
Drink deep and listen
How the music weaves lovely cloth and strong.

The wanderer of the night looks
To the stars that come up in his eyes
And drinks of them, and his feet are well placed.

Canto Sixteen

As you would have others do unto you
Do you even so unto them.
Keep this rich extract
With you always.
To the unjust turn
And give justice even as you would
Give straightness to a twisted limb,
And to the harsh show strength of mildness.
To the hot temper be cool.
To the cold
Give warmth, and to the false truth.
This is the beginning of things among us.

Canto Seventeen

Through the rounds of days and
Time it comes that they who
Would slash the sky slash themselves
And sharpen the edge of fate.
But they who go patiently do most.
The listener hears the scraps and cries
As part of a great song and goes steadily.
And his time is good.
And happiness moves among
The cool columns of hours
Barely noticed, as though
It were engaged forever.

Canto Eighteen

Some go forth and do a great work,
Let them have the praise for it.
And some do excellent
Works, let them have their praise.
And some do beautiful and good
Things, surely they are due no less.
Yet the most of what is good
Is plain and is done in the letterless
Days and not proclaimed Here is it.
And so is the praise plain
Or croaked out in bits or not at all.
Or threading a mute trail
Through afterdays of forgotten time.
It suddenly pulls in the moistening
Grip of a babe,
Or speaks in a long aged grasp.
Then sing to the day
To this day in its own,
With largeness and ease of heart sing,
Freely and trusting sing on,
Sing to this day.
The day will not be silent to you.

Part III

Heard in the Night

A Nearness

The Night

The hour has come.
Let us take of the sweetness of the night
And in our light breathing
Thoughts and fresh remembrances
Glide free of the grasp of things.
Though hid away the stars may be
Guessed in their steady orbs.
Sounds that would disturb muffle up
And become lost from idling sense.
Neither breath nor heart is heard.
How good it is but to be
And let the slow sweep of the sea-bathed
World round and turn
As dusty day drifts off.
The soft lustrous light, sometimes seen
Harsh and crossed, melts
As the waxen glow of dusk roses.
We enter the wondrous stream.
As the current enfolds and cradles
No word need be uttered,
Our thoughts float free.
Brushing silently over the lips
Unnamed wishes and hopes rise, turn
And sway
As flowers nod in murmuring air.
The crestless waves of the night's passing
Wake roll and curl and glide on

Turning away the outer globe as velvet sheds
A waterdrop or a drop of quicksilver.
How freely life floods now,
Seeming here to amass its pools
And fill for all the flow.
We float at ease.
What comes will come, be a while
And go again.
The tides hold distant sway and are welcome
For they work and tug with us.
The world is well enough that it holds
This quiet session when we may become composed
And ravel out our troubles with our delights
And our hopes.
We do not come to ask nor to receive
But to approach and perhaps to touch.
What passes in this gentle
Existence cannot be seized
For it flows as the ample stream
Of our fullest life.
Now all the great heaving mass must
Lay itself down and take a breath,
The heavy brute no less than
The exhausted one of delicate virtue.
Let us whisper in their ears
Encouragements and happy ways.
So many are poor in them
And dry and cracked within.
We shall give clear waters to them

For the waters of this hour are better than wine
And go as balm upon the sores of the breast.
They will revive as drooping flowers
And turn about and wonder whence they come.
How beautiful are the moments of this night
Passing over the memory.
Time's measures dip and spill with refreshing drops
Falling numberless through golden boughs.
The air of the night steals its gossamers,
It rises and falls as the breath of the lake
Wreathing and wisping this little isle,
Breathing over dull embers and temples.
Our presence fuses and dissolves,
Effortlessly roiling and subliming.
Come, gather strength and come with us.
Our way is longer but
It is more beautiful and happier.
We call to you softly. Surely you hear.
Suddenly in the midst of an act
You stop and lay aside your things to listen.
Come, let us go together.
Do not fear. We shall be faithful.
One falling, another shall rise.
Always renewing, constantly and ceaselessly
Renewing and quietly unfolding.
Imperceptible transformations, slowing moving,
Soundlessly and wondrously receiving
The charge, pouring forth marvelously.
Measured according to all times,

Not by these times alone,
And by the green futurities bearing
The fruit of us.
This hour is but a breath on the way,
The mute observance
Of the settling compass needle.
A sip at the spring,
A glance over the shoulder,
A few words with the strongest and surest,
Uttering hardly a sound.

The Charge of Life

Who will wed you, gentle girl,
A lover only?
A passion husband?
A blinding bull of the night
Whose leaping charge will seep
Into the marrow of your child?
Know him.
Have mercy on the bewildered babe
You heave out upon the world.
A fate hangs in your seeing eye.

In the Troubled Hour

In the troubled hour
I hurry to you
Lying pale in the fevered storm.
We rise through all, my being
Wrapped about your trembling body,
My cool cheek pressed to yours hot.
Here, here I am,
It is my cheek with yours,
They are my eyes that shine for yours,
They are my hands that press for yours,
I shall keep with you
And succor you and comfort you,
And I shall stir up nourishment in your blood.

Now Unto Mercy

And I come in the flutter
Of the broken wing.
And in the scream of the torn
Soldier I come,
Vibrate in your memory.
And again I whisper in the look
Of the cornered breadwinner,
I peer out of his eyes.
He is frightened and I speak out of him.
Behold! I come in the snuffle
Of the smothering child,
In the anguish of the amputated lovers,
In the moan of the cancer host,
And in the still.
I come to be with you
And to rise up in your troubled thoughts.
Keep me always.

Blanket in the Sun

I was lucky.
I didn't make a sound when my arm
Was torn out at the roots.
And the hole broken through my cheek
Gave me air.
And when a piece of my side was
Flung into the bushes still buttoned in shirt
And my eyes crushed like frozen
Strawberries in milk,
What could I say?
Can you put in a word for me?
They're sending me home to the family
But they won't know what to say.

Reply to Misfortune

He threw back his head and laughed
The laugh that goes roaring and rocking
Down the highways of the sky
The laugh that rides
The bounding lion of courage
The laugh that flings
Despair to the ground
With the back of the hand
The laugh that spills all over
Destiny like an insolent boy.
There he stood
Laughing the great wide laugh of a master
Rolling it out
On the roller coaster
That rides the plunge and laughs.

At Last

It is ended.
Not all the wailing ever wrung,
Nor all the tears heavy salted
And swallowed, nor the fondled memories,
Nor all the wishes wished and rued
Down long stares of blankness
Can call it back.
Nor shall there end
The unguessed beginnings
Brought in the lap of the tides.

The One Composed

Cool and composed
I stand beside you,
I heard what you heard,
I see the trembling of your hand,
And I hear the trembling of your throat,
Yet I am cool and composed:
For there is something more to be heard,
Resting quiet in the memory.

From Slumbers and Depths

Some teach you lowliness
And helplessness
And a deep crying
For what you cannot find,
Stirring a watery stew for suckle
When you are weak with hungers.
But these lines are not to cut
The sinews of your spirit
Nor break your will across another,
But to midwife gristle
And a happy power
Amid the heaves of pain and joys
And to sing for your springs
In the wondrous river of life
Tumbling, deep running and constantly pooling.
With lines and bits of these verses
They may be waked and brought up
From sleeping and depths where they lie
Part formed or forgot.
There is no need to strain eagerly,
The cradle of the deep rocks at will.
Nor be alarmed when something
Slips from your grasp and
Disappears to become part of the rest.

Nor Eagle nor Lamb

Often have you been
Told to be proud,
And many times admonished
To humbleness.
Now it is time to advance,
Not one nor the other will do.
Be neither proud nor humble,
Nor poison nor antidote,
Nor eagle nor lamb,
But you, unfolding and worthy.

This to Answer

Must I shock you to make you listen?
Must I tell you unfathomable lies
To make you believe?
Must I crush your hopes
To make you tender?
Or do you recognize the signs
Of simple truths?
What I tell you has no fashion
And no deception,
It will wear well with you,
And it will bring you
Close to the vitals of your life.

The Fisher

Here is my many-latticed net
So patiently woven and pliant.
Take it with you. And now and then,
As you walk the sands of the sea
Fling it wide away wheeling and skimming
The briny diamond-showering breeze.
What you take from the surge and the crests
Will be live and whole
And dripping with water and life.
Froth and seaweed and perhaps
Some curious pieces of dark
Dead wood may come too.
But there will not be the deathly
Precision of the sharp pointing spear.

The Mighty and the Gentle

The gentle have powers to draw
The loves of peace into the mighty
As naturally as sweet passes tooth,
For they know them,
And even so are the mighty
Wont to have need for them
And be in their own peril for them.

Honeycomb

Her slender silver face
Lives in moon-stillness.
She gazes long,
Hungers some,
Partakes modestly,
Listens, chuckles, ponders,
Storing and delving a honeycomb of life
Beneath a pale tranquil surface.
Some say laugh, enjoy yourself, be like us.
Another says don't laugh, enjoy yourself,
Be like you.

As Strange Music

The beauty of a homely face is withheld
As strange music.
Sensed in the flash of a moment
It wheels and vanishes in the wilderness
To peep out from pools and crags.
Sometimes gliding from shade to shade
Wisping by a memory,
Sometimes rambling off lost and wild
Down swirling mists to fall
Without a sound,
Sometimes startling, rushing out
From hollows and folds to leap
Naked on the open plain —
And in that instant crushed by light.
And sometimes remaining near,
Wrapped in so little as a smile or air.

Leave

Will you stay with me a while,
Then I'll go.
We'll walk a ways and talk
And say things we never say.
And we'll listen to the clattered
Sighing of the streets
And the distant horn
And wish we could go on.
Then we'll sit down
But I'll not tell you how it was.
We will look away
And see what we always see
In the way of strangers.
I will tell you who I am,
You'll not know but does it matter.
Then we'll swallow our crusts and feel time
Stumble and wait.
You may think me gentle
But will not know.

The Tree

Standing alone under the bare fists
Of the weathers, baked with heats,
Dried with droughts, coddled with dews,
Chilled and cracked of branches
And all shrieked upon
By the meanest winds,
The tree stands and gives.
With time the fair returns
And the tree sends forth
Its tender hopes and bines,
The good season is kind to them
And bathes them and warms and feeds them,
There peacefully waving on the gentle airs
The young greens weave out their life
To a plan of simple needs.
Then returns the time
When the sun becomes distant,
The voices of nature crack
And lose their warble,
And the sky is torn
And whipped over crusted earth,
Again the tree is shaken
And rawly tried from limb to root
By lashing bitter winds.
They blast upon its heart

And wrestle it and twist its limbs.
But the tree has a suppleness,
It stands strong, deep-rooted
In the earth.

Spoken for a Child

Teach me the letters
That I may see
Beyond my sight,
Teach me the hand
That I may speak
Beyond my voice,
But plant in me
Deep, half as deep
As your love,
A discipline of self,
That I may not be
Tormented by myself,
That I may go safely
Through vinegar seas and sweet syrups.

The Crab

See, the crab!
How gnarled and strangely formed.
Feel the hard shell
And the intricate designs.
Such sensitive feelers.
He is testy and shy.
Come, he will bite you,
Or more gladly skitter away.
But wait.
Perhaps he is the most interesting one of all.

Lockless

Lay up good riches within your brows,
Then may they be close to hand
And sure to keep,
Such a chest is not hid in the dark
Nor made heavy and ponderous,
Jauntily it carries your fortune
Among glitter or ruin
Among power and crush
Through shallows and black forests,
A treasure box never lost.

Means and Ends

There is the talk of the means
And the talk of the ends,
That the means are all
And the ends are all.
Yet how can means fulfill
If they point to vacant ends?
And how are ends human ends
If the means degrade men and women?
Often means beget ends
No less than ends beget means,
For means are as well
The beginnings of ends.
Nor is it told in the balance
Of weighty matters.
For surely the time of life
Is spun out with means
Seeming to lack a heft of ends.
And how often is some mountainous
Coil of tangled means
Light in balance with an infant's breath.
What of a song?
It is weightless, yet it fills
And rises with meaning
Being means and end in one.
So the making of life
Is with the means and the ends,
Wound and woven each to each,

As the vine entwines and weaves its being
With moist root and curling tendril
The podding bloom within
And the tipmost bloom and reach.

A Country Walk

Moving into simplicity
With careless tosses,
Hearing no small doubts or questions,
Feeling the melt of vibrations into waves,
The fresh bright air folding
Over hands and face,
The earth firm and trustworthy under foot,
The open fields basking and rolling,
The slender spears
Of grass lithely swaying
And floating up sweet smells,
The great tree weaving and gliding,
The water sounds of the leaves
Swishing and rustling.
The gurgle and bound ahead
Of the pebble,
The leathered toe pressing the pebble
Flush into the moist earth,
The fulfillment
Coming out of this simple act.
The dibbling in the moss-banked
Run of the water,
The flow of thoughts
Into the waters and juices of the earth,
The bobbing about and cleansing of them,
And the floating away
In wondrous curling eddies.

A stone crystal winks
Flares and dims.
Slowly silently
An easy silent churning rolls up the puffs
And veils of the heavens.
The last tardy cloud vanishes with the wisps.
An inner balance is almost heard.

Cry Beloved

Save me, O save me my land and my people.
The land turns bitter and my people are like lemmings,
They race one another and build on each other's heads.
The air and the water sicken and there is
War with nature. Save me my wild rivers and splendid surf
Where crowding thoughts can ride up free and foam
And chase. Save me clear lakes where I can see my nakedness.
Keep for me mantles of rich earth dense with coloring minerals
And peeping flowers, broad belts of green, and fragrant forests.
Let the boughs breathe a slender air
And the needles of the pine be clean, to spice lingering
Walks with refreshments and incensed depths.
Save us from mad crowds that peacefully trample life to death,
And the traffic roar that sets tight-wound inner ears to beg
For a severance or a deadening draught.
O my people, will the hot breath of consuming numbers
Make us a wasteland? Let us have comely parks, fair cities
And gardens to smile at us, happy places where a child can
Wander over thrusting sprigs and spongy turf falling sometimes
Unawares into the preserving rhythms of the earth.
Save us town air clear enough to wish in
Where hungry darts of sun may slip clean among the trees,
Bushy hills climbing up from herded hours, some old dirt roads
To plow and smooth with twenty toes, rough barked trees splitting
With ripe age and heat, the virginal sculpture of cracked rocks,
Cool undisturbed beds of pebbled sand filtering their trickled
Rillets where we may rise our eyes in liquid day and watch

The sparkling finger press water into tiny greens.
Vast pure plains of magic hues to whirl and dance out
Dull imagination, the fresh combing breeze clean with the glitter
And bite of distant peaks, gentle hidden valleys to stay a while
And pry into mossy banks and light-freckled groves.
Ah for that little moment to look up dizzy in the tower
Of a giant pine and catch the yawl of black cloud scudding
And steaming off to a sunny death. Lost, forever lost?
Then come down to the sea of scalloped isles
And brown-buffed beaches, past duck-bobbing inlets
        and soft weedy
Shores where fierce-eyed herons preen their glossy plumage,
There at last to sink into the warm lap of the blue-girdled
Cove so faintly stirred with the plop of feathered breasts
And the nudge and spin of fish at feeding. Lost, ah lost, this too?
Then look through tangled asphalt ribbons, hot white slabs,
The drugging murk of steel shafts and stacks
And car-blown shrubs. Not there, not there?
Look, then, down the silent reeling street where
Trees dig their twisted feet into what's left
And drop sere leafy notes for help.

Repose

My hands are folded
And my brow is light,
And I lie in the
Lap of content,
For this day
I have believed
What I have done,
And now is the sweet night that follows.

Through Eternity

Keep a part of me
That we do not completely die,
That something of us may live on
Through eternity.